D0613923

Table of Contents

Boxer Puppies	3
Photo Glossary	15
Index	16
About the Author	16

Rourke Educational Media
A Division of Carson Dellosa Education
rourkeeducationalmedia.com

Can you find these words?

explore

hair

puppies

swats

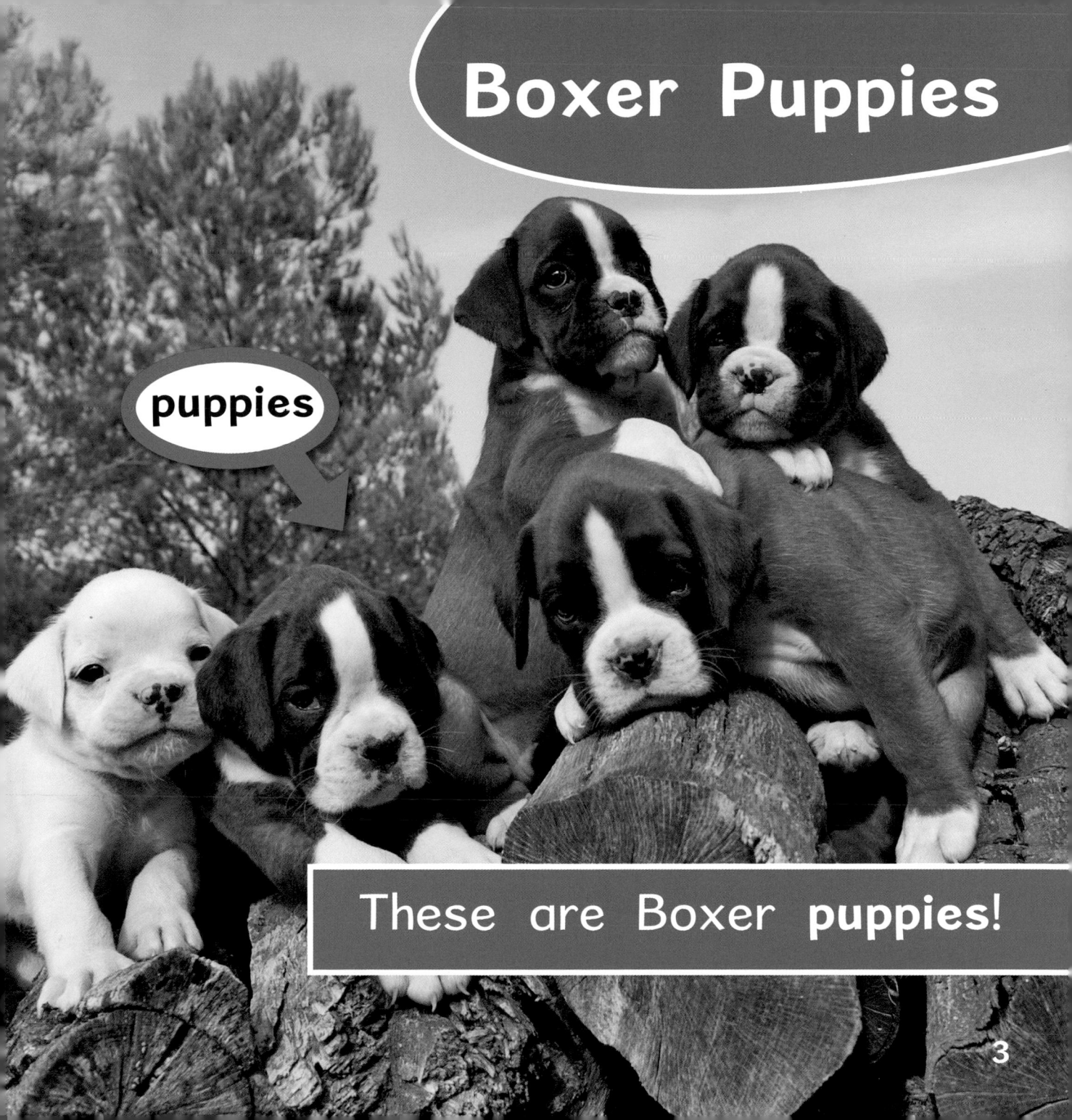
Boxer Puppies
puppies
These are Boxer puppies!

What do Boxer puppies look like?

Their faces have a square shape.

They have short **hair.**

What do Boxer puppies act like?

They are curious.
They like to **explore**.

They want to play.

This puppy **swats** at a friend.

They need people.

They are part of the family.

Did you find these words?

They like to **explore**.

They have short **hair**.

These are Boxer **puppies**!

This puppy **swats** at a friend.

Photo Glossary

explore (ik-SPLOR): To travel and look around to find things.

hair (hair): Thin strands that grow from the body.

puppies (PUHP-eez): Dogs that are young and not fully grown.

swats (swahts): Hits with a quick blow.

Index

curious 9
faces 5
family 13
friend 11
people 12
play 10

About the Author

Hailey Scragg is a writer from Ohio. She loves all puppies, especially her puppy, Abe! She likes taking him on long walks in the park.

© 2020 Rourke Educational Media

All rights reserved. No part of this book may be reproduced or utilized in any form or by any means, electronic or mechanical including photocopying, recording, or by any information storage and retrieval system without permission in writing from the publisher.

www.rourkeeducationalmedia.com

PHOTO CREDITS: cover: ©2windspa, ©manley099 (bone); back cover: ©zhobla91 (inset), ©Naddiya (pattern); pages 2, 3, 8-9, 14, 15: ©cynoclub; pages 4-5: ©JLSnader; pages 2, 6-7, 14, 15: ©Astrid Schur; pages 2, 10-11, 14, 15: ©Betty4240; pages 12-13: ©lewkmiller

Edited by: Kim Thompson
Cover and interior design by: Janine Fisher

Library of Congress PCN Data
Boxer Puppies / Hailey Scragg
(Top Puppies)
ISBN 978-1-73162-873-2 (hard cover)(alk. paper)
ISBN 978-1-73162-872-5 (soft cover)
ISBN 978-1-73162-874-9 (e-Book)
ISBN 978-1-73163-345-3 (ePub)
Library of Congress Control Number: 2019944973

Printed in the United States of America,
North Mankato, Minnesota